Heart to Heart with God

Six Ways to Empower Your Prayer Life

Heart to Heart with God

Six Ways to Empower Your Prayer Life

Deacon Ralph Torrelli

the WORD
among us®
press

The Word Among Us Press
9639 Doctor Perry Road
Ijamsville, Maryland 21754
www.wordamongus.org

12 11 10 09 08 1 2 3 4 5

ISBN: 978-1-59325-125-3

Nihil Obstat: Very Reverend T. Dominick Fullam
Censor

Imprimatur: Most Reverend Thomas J. Rodi
Bishop of Biloxi
September 6, 2007

Unless otherwise noted, Scripture passages contained herein are from the New Revised Standard Version Bible: Catholic Edition, copyright © 1989, 1993 Division of Christian Education of the National Council of the Churches of Christ in the United States. All rights reserved. Used with permission.

Excerpts from the English translation of the Catechism of the Catholic Church for use in the United States of America, copyright © 1994, United States Catholic Conference, Inc. – Libreria Editrice Vaticana. Used with permission.

Cover design by David Crosson

Made and printed in the United States of America

Library of Congress Cataloging-in-Publication Data

Torrelli, Ralph.
Heart to heart with God : six ways to empower your prayer life / Ralph Torrelli.
p. cm.
ISBN 978-1-59325-125-3 (alk. paper)
1. Prayer--Christianity. I. Title.
BV210.3.T67 2008
248.3'2--dc22
2007040505

Contents

Welcome to
The Word Among Us
Keys to the Bible

Have you ever lost your keys? Everyone seems to have at least one "lost keys" story to tell. Maybe you had to break a window of your house or wait for the auto club to let you into your car. Whatever you had to do probably cost you—in time, energy, money, or all three. Keys are definitely important items to have on hand!

The guides in The Word Among Us Keys to the Bible series are meant to provide you with a handy set of keys that can "unlock" the treasures of the Scriptures for you. Scripture is God's living word. Within its pages we meet the Lord. So as we study and meditate on Scripture and unlock its many treasures, we discover the riches it contains—and in the process, we grow in intimacy with God.

Since 1982, The Word Among Us magazine has helped Catholics develop a deeper relationship with the Lord through daily meditations that bring the Scriptures to life. More than ever, Catholics today desire to read and pray with the Scriptures, and many have begun to form small faith-sharing groups to explore the Bible together.

We recently conducted a survey among our magazine readers to learn what they wanted in a Catholic Bible study. The many enthusiastic responses we received led us to create this new series. Readers told us they are looking for easy-to-understand, faith-filled materials that approach Scripture from a clearly Catholic perspective. Moreover, they want a Bible study that shows them how they can apply what they learn from Scripture to their everyday lives. And since most of our readers lead busy lives, they asked for sessions that they can complete in an hour or two.

On the basis of the survey results, we set out to design a simple, easy-to-use Bible study guide that is also challenging and thought provoking. We hope that this guide fulfills those admittedly ambitious goals. We are confident, however, that taking the time to go through this guide—whether by yourself, with a friend, or in a small group—will be a worthwhile endeavor that will bear fruit in your life.

How to Use the Guides in This Series

The study guides in the Keys to the Bible series are divided into six sessions that each deal with a particular aspect of the topic. Before starting the first session, take the time to read the introduction, which sets the stage for the sessions that follow.

Whether you use this guide for personal reflection and study, as part of a faith-sharing group, or as an aid in your prayer time, be sure to begin each session with prayer. Ask God to open his word to you and to speak to you personally. Read each Scripture passage slowly and carefully. Then, take as much time as you need to meditate on the passage and pursue any thoughts it brings to mind. When you are ready, move on to the accompanying commentary, which offers various insights into the text.

Two sets of questions are included in each session to help you "mine" the Scripture passage and discover its relevance to your life. Those under the heading "Understand!" focus on the text itself and help you grasp what it means. Occasionally a question allows for a variety of answers and is meant to help you explore the passage from several angles. "Grow!" questions are intended to elicit a personal response by helping you examine your life in light of the values and truths that you uncover through your study of the Scripture passage and its setting. Under the headings "Reflect!" and "Act!" we offer suggestions to help you respond concretely to the challenges posed by the passage.

Finally, pertinent quotations from the Fathers of the Church, insights from contemporary writers, and personal testimonies appear throughout each session. Coupled with relevant selections from the *Catechism of the Catholic Church* and information about the history, geography, and culture of first-century Palestine, these selections (called "In the Spotlight") add new layers of understanding and insight to your study.

As is true with any other learning resource, you will benefit the most from this study by writing your answers to the questions in the spaces provided. The simple act of writing can help you formulate your thoughts more clearly—and will also give you a record of your reflections and spiritual growth that you can return to in the future to see how much God has accomplished in your life. End your reading or study with a prayer thanking God for what you have learned—and ask the Holy Spirit to guide you in living out the call you have been given as a Christian in the world today.

Although the Scripture passages to be studied and the related verses for your reflection are printed in full in each guide (from the New Revised Standard Version: Catholic Edition), you will find it helpful to have a Bible on hand for looking up other passages and cross-references or for comparing different translations.

The format of the guides in The Word Among Us Keys to the Bible series is especially well suited for use in small groups. Some recommendations and practical tips for using this guide in a Bible discussion group are offered on pages 103–106.

As you use this book, may the Lord increase your faith in him so that you know, without a shadow of a doubt, that his love for you exceeds all bounds, that he listens to your prayers, and that he wants an intimate relationship with you that grows stronger each day of your life.

The Word Among Us Press

Introduction
The Effectiveness of Heartfelt Prayer

Prayer and Scripture study are essential for anyone who aspires to grow in holiness. This Bible study, focusing on six attitudes and actions you can take to empower your prayer life, builds on that principle. It will help you draw inspiration and momentum for prayer by placing you at the scene of powerful biblical encounters and events.

In this guide, you can imagine yourself as a bystander on the dusty roads of Palestine, listening to Bartimaeus calling out to Jesus and watching Jesus respond by healing him of his blindness. Or, you can wait for the coming of the Holy Spirit with the apostles and Mary in the upper room. You can be a witness at the scene at the Beautiful Gate of the Temple, when Peter and John healed the lame beggar by praying in the name of Jesus. Perhaps you can reflect on how Moses felt as he pleaded with God not to destroy the Israelites for worshipping the golden calf.

"Prayer Warriors" for Our Age

Biblical history overflows with incidences of God's life-changing intervention in human affairs because men and women "prayer warriors" believed without equivocation in the effectiveness of heartfelt prayer. My prayer is for the Lord to raise empowered prayer warriors in our age with a longing to continue this history in and through themselves and others. It is a history as old as creation and as new as the moment you picked up this book. Even before the age of literacy, generations of believers told biblical stories of great heroes of faith. Books, movies, the Internet, and other forms of media aid parents, grandparents, and teachers in sharing these same stories today. Such enthusiastic sharing encourages us to follow the prayer attitudes and actions recorded in past times.

In the Rite of Christian Initiation of Adults (RCIA), there is a point at which candidates consider a saint whose name they will adopt as their confirmation name. Each candidate is encouraged to prayerfully research the saint's biography. Enthusiasm is contagious and faith stirred when the candidates announce the saint they have chosen and the reasons for their choice. In their discovery of a person who has triumphed over adversity in circumstances similar to their own, another story is told, and history is continued.

Finding Models in Saints and Biblical Heroes

All of us can find a biblical character or a saint whose life is a model of what we would like ours to be. When God significantly touches someone's life, there is often a powerful period of grace that follows. At such times, our prayer life flourishes with power, confidence, and effectiveness.

The patriarchs Abraham, Isaac, Jacob, and Moses were nomads living in tents with their families who had no land or nation to call their own. The God of creation burst into their lives with a promise of love, care, prosperity, and faithfulness, and these men and their followers were never the same. They saw kingdoms fall and rise, people destroyed and given new life, and personal and communal responsibility established. Prayer and faith were their foundations, and empowerment was the result of their newly found relationship with the living God. Prophets, kings, and judges succeeded these patriarchs in proclaiming the will of God to a people formerly lost and confused, without hope or promise in their lives. These chosen instruments of God wielded awesome power to defeat enemies, to raise the dead, and to heal the sick (see 1 Kings 18:20-40; 2 Kings 4:32-37). They admonished and comforted people in a continuous cycle of separation from and restoration to God.

Such a special time of grace and power also began for the apostles when they responded to the call of Jesus. In their desire to learn about his power, love, and prayer life, they asked him, "Lord, teach us to pray" (Luke 11:1). To these simple men Jesus gave the power to forgive sins, preach the good news, and heal the sick (see Luke 9:1-7). They were charged with building the church and passing on the faith to future generations (see Acts 1:1-8). In the face of hostility, imprisonments, and deprivation, prayer gave the apostles hope and courage. Through it all, Jesus prayed for them, with them, in them, and through them. Vibrant prayer was the foundation of their daily existence, leading them to victory in overcoming obstacles, setbacks, and persecutions.

Restoring the Power

What has happened to this special time of grace and power? Is it lost in the past? Must we minimally plod along in our faith, at times barely hanging in there, with the absence of a clear assurance of who God is, how much he loves us, and the awesome power he is willing to use for our benefit? Are we to rely only on rote prayer that can be beneficial but may rob us of the intimacy and spontaneity that comprise a passionate relationship with God? In *Heart to Heart with God*, you will study and reflect on biblical heroes of the faith whose attitudes and actions made their petitions powerful and effective. As we uncover those attitudes and dispositions of prayer, we will be inspired to adopt the same attitudes in our own life of prayer.

Some people view prayer as a psychological activity whereas others reduce it to a ritual of words and simple postures. Still others regard prayer as an occupation that is incompatible with all the other things they have to do; they don't have time for it. In this study, we identify attitudes that stifle the power of prayer—such as self-centeredness, misguided desires, or busyness—and offer guidance to overcome these obstacles.

Positive Attitudes of Prayer

We stress the positive attitudes of prayer. We pray the desire of our heart, because the God of love dwells in our hearts. We pray persistently to emulate the Lord's faithfulness in never giving up on us. We pray boldly, expectantly, and specifically because Jesus and the Old Testament heroes of our faith proved the effectiveness of such prayer attitudes. We pray with the armor of God to confront the spiritual and temporal struggles of daily life and offer dispositions to be victorious in those battles.

The experience of prayer teaches us that faith rests on God's action. God initiates, inspires, and preserves faith in the heart of the believer through an intimate personal and communal union. Our cooperation with God's action leads to a prayer life that glorifies the Lord in his plan of salvation and allows us to be co-laborers in making that plan successful. If our prayer unites us with that of Jesus', we obtain all that we ask in his name.

The exciting and power-filled adventure of this Bible study now awaits you. As you move through each session, pray that the Holy Spirit will create, heighten, and continue in you the contagious intimacy of a passionate, personal relationship with the Lord. May your cooperation with God's will help you to embrace that special time of grace and power for years to come!

Deacon Ralph Torrelli

To the God Who Never Gives Up on Me

Luke 18:1-8

[1]Jesus told them a parable about their need to pray always and not to lose heart. [2]He said, "In a certain city there was a judge who neither feared God nor had respect for people. [3]In that city there was a widow who kept coming to him saying, 'Grant me justice against my opponent.' [4]For a while he refused; but later he said to himself, 'Though I have no fear of God and no respect for anyone, [5]yet because this widow keeps bothering me, I will grant her justice, so that she may not wear me out by continually coming.'" [6]And the Lord said, "Listen to what the unjust judge says. [7]And will not God grant justice to his chosen ones who cry to him day and night? Will he delay long in helping them? [8]I tell you, he will quickly grant justice to them. And yet, when the Son of Man comes, will he find faith on earth?"

The purpose of Jesus' parable is clearly stated in the first sentence of this passage: the need to pray always. No matter how grim our circumstances, we should never give up praying. Whether we have prayed once, twice, or countless times, and even if we find ourselves disheartened, we need an attitude of persistence, girded by obedience, to pray again and again.

The woman in this parable had three major liabilities that hindered her from obtaining justice. First, she was poor and could not afford to pay a bribe to the corrupt judge. Second, she was a woman. Women in first-century Palestine were second-class citizens, little better off than slaves, and had no power, authority, or influence. Third, she was a widow. In legal or public matters, a married woman's husband would have to speak for her; a widow could not act as her own advocate.

Blinded by his corruption, the judge was cold and calculating and refused to recognize the woman's plight. In view of her predicament, it would be perfectly logical to conclude that obtaining justice in this case would be nearly impossible. But Jesus challenges his listeners to consider that perfect logic could mask imperfect faith. Faith looks beyond what is seen and heard and persists with a desire of what can be. Jesus then offers the prescription for hope in the face of a hopeless dilemma. When we have made every effort within our power to correct a situation and its solution is beyond our control, we can surrender the burden and turn it over to God through persistent prayer.

The habit of persistent prayer takes the focus off the obstacle (in this case, the unjust judge) and places it on the solution (our just God). The judge of corruption and the God of justice are a study in contrasts. The judge cannot be trusted, is unjust, merciless, uncompassionate, and must be coerced or threatened to act. God can be trusted (see Psalm 62:8), is just (see Isaiah 45:21), is merciful (see Lamentations 3:22-23), and loves us unconditionally (see John 3:16).

The story also implies the following progression of spiritual growth: need causes us to pray, persistence in prayer strengthens our relationship with God, and intimacy with God leads to increased faith, which often results in a favorable answer to our prayer. Need is the primary motivator that drives us to God, whether it be illness, troubled relationships, job security, financial problems, or something else. We seek God and communicate our need through communal and personal prayer. Persistence in prayer breaks through the wall we sometimes build to distance ourselves from God and stirs a desire to be more deeply intimate with our creator. Intimacy with God is our love-response to his love-initiative and builds confidence, trust, and a strengthened faith. Answered prayer provides the courage to repeat the cycle when another need arises.

The final verses assure us that God will be our advocate when there is no one to defend our cause. He will surely and quickly hear and answer every prayer, for our good, in accord with his purpose and plan for our lives. We can rely on a loving God who has an eager, listening ear and a compassionate heart.

Understand!

1. Luke introduces Jesus' parable by saying it is about their "need to pray always and not to lose heart" (18:1). How might this parable have helped Jesus' listeners not to lose heart?

_____

_____

_____

_____

_____

_____

_____

2. Why might Jesus have chosen to use a widow to make his point? What character traits does she exhibit in this parable?

_____

_____

_____

_____

_____

_____

_____

3. What is the role of the unjust judge in this parable? Why do you think Jesus said, "Listen to what the unjust judge says" (18:6)?

_____

_____

_____

_____

_____

_____

_____

4. What eventually motivated the judge to deliver a just decision in the woman's favor? In what ways does the justice issued by the judge differ from God's justice?

_____

_____

_____

_____

_____

_____

_____

5. Jesus' closing words in the parable are, "When the Son of Man comes, will he find faith on earth?" Why do you think he ended with such a question?

_____

_____

_____

_____

_____

_____

▶ In the Spotlight
The Legal System in First-Century Palestine

Although the Jews had a system of arbitration, they almost never used it. Instead, they took disputes to the elders, who would decide the outcome of the conflict. If they deemed arbitration necessary, there were always three judges chosen: one by the plaintiff, one by the defendant, and one independently appointed. The judge in this parable was not a Jewish judge.

He was likely a paid magistrate appointed either by King Herod or by the Romans. Such judges were notoriously corrupt. Unless a person had influence and money to bribe his or her way to a verdict, there was little hope of getting the case settled. The people called these judges *Dayyaneh Gezeloth*, which in Hebrew means "robber judges."

Grow!

1. What negative attitudes and thoughts are we tempted to entertain when we feel that God is either distant or silent in prayer? What do you think might be a way to counter such attitudes?

_____

_____

_____

_____

_____

_____

_____

_____

2. Look back at a time in your life when an important need drove you to prayer. What effect did your prayer have on your relationship with God?

_____

_____

_____

_____

_____

_____

_____

3. When you pray, how often do you consciously surrender your request to God? What might prevent you from fully surrendering your burdens to the Lord?

_____

_____

_____

_____

_____

_____

4. What job, family, social, civic, or academic situation can you recall where you have succeeded in your purpose because you persevered? Share a particular incident where your perseverance with God worked out as well.

_____

_____

_____

_____

_____

_____

5. How can the promises of Jesus in Scripture strengthen your resolve to persist in prayer? What Scripture verses might help you the next time you are tempted to give up praying?

_____

_____

_____

_____

_____

_____

▶ In the Spotlight
"The Absent Lover"

Imagine telling your best friend, "I met this wonderful person and have fallen deeply in love. Of course, we see each other only one day a week, and only for one hour, and only on those days when I show up, which may not always be every week. When we do get together, we are in the presence of hundreds of other people, so I am often distracted by what is going on around me." By this time, your friend will scream, "Stop! I've heard enough! Are you losing your mind? How can you call this a relationship?"

Does the description of the absent lover resemble in any way your relationship with the Lord? Is it possible for a deep and personal faith relationship to develop if you have little quality prayer, study, worship, or reflection time? God wants and deserves more of our time and attention. Develop a consistent and persistent routine of personal prayer, intercessory prayer, prayers of praise and thanksgiving, meditative prayer, and spontaneous prayer from the heart, talking to God as you would a best friend.

Reflect!

1. Reflect on the ways you resemble the "absent lover" in your relationship with God. How can you spend more quality time with your lover, God?

2. The following passages can help increase your understanding of the parable of the woman and the corrupt judge:

> [Jesus said,] "Suppose one of you has a friend and you go to him at midnight and say, 'Friend, lend me three loaves of bread; for a friend of mine has arrived, and I

have nothing to set before him,' And he answers from within, 'Do not bother me; the door has already been locked, and my children are with me in bed; I cannot get up and give you anything.' I tell you, even though he will not get up and give him anything because he is his friend, at least because of his persistence he will get up and give him whatever he needs. So I say to you, Ask and it will be given to you; search and you will find; knock and the door will be opened for you."

—Luke 11:5-9

The LORD said, "How great is the outcry against Sodom and Gomorrah and how very grave is their sin!" . . . Then Abraham . . . said, "Will you indeed sweep away the righteous with the wicked? Suppose there are fifty righteous within the city; will you then sweep away the place and not forgive it for the fifty righteous who are in it? Far be it from you to do such a thing, to slay the righteous with the wicked! . . . Shall not the Judge of all the earth do what is just?" And the LORD said, "If I find at Sodom fifty righteous in the city, I will forgive the whole place for their sake." Abraham answered, ". . . Suppose five of the fifty righteous are lacking? Will you destroy the whole city for lack of five?" And he said, I will not destroy it if I find forty-five there." . . . "Suppose forty are found there." He answered, "For the sake of forty I will not do it." Then he said, . . . "Suppose thirty are found there." He answered, "I will not do it, if I find thirty there." He said, . . . "Suppose twenty are found there." He answered, "For the sake of twenty I will not destroy it." Then he said, "Oh do not let the Lord be angry if I speak just once more. Suppose ten are found there." He answered, "For the sake of ten I will not destroy it."

—Genesis 18:20, 23-32

Devote yourselves to prayer, keeping alert in it with thanksgiving.

—Colossians 4:2

Incline your ear, O LORD, and answer me,
    for I am poor and needy.
Preserve my life, for I am devoted to you;
    save your servant who trusts in you. . . .
    for to you do I cry all day long. . . .
Give ear, O LORD, to my prayer.

—Psalm 86:1-3, 6

Do not lag in zeal, be ardent in spirit, serve the Lord. Rejoice in hope, be patient in suffering, persevere in prayer.

—Romans 12:11-12

▶In the Spotlight
"Pray without Ceasing"

As we look through the New Testament and other Greek literature at the use of the Greek adverb translated "without ceasing" (1 Thessalonians 5:17 = Pray without ceasing) we understand the sense of the term as a literal praying without stopping. This type of prayer would be uninterrupted verbal prayer by the believer. As practiced in the past, this type of verbal prayer continues all through the day—if not in physical utterance by the person himself, then by a mediator. Stories are told of monasteries full of constant prayer. Out of each monk's monetary allowance, a certain portion was set aside for payment to a brother to pray while the monk could not physically utter prayer, such as during sleep. The brothers helped one another to "pray without ceasing" by praying on behalf of one another as part of their ministry. With this system, so it

was thought, sweet fragrances of prayer were uttered unceasingly—as a constant recurrence or without interruption.
—Henri J. M. Nouwen, "The Call to Unceasing Prayer"

Act!

Do you know someone who has not persevered in the practice of his or her faith? Pray before you act, then contact one person this week to invite to Mass with you or to a church program that may interest him or her. Make it as convenient as possible by offering a ride, buying the person's ticket, or some other generous act. Be creative.

Do you know any widows, widowers, or single parents who may be lonely and need someone to lift their spirits and encourage their prayer and faith life? Pray persistently for them, and in the next few weeks, find ways to reach out to them.

▶In the Spotlight
Wisdom from the Saints

There are some favors that the Almighty does not grant either the first, or the second, or the third time you ask him, because he wishes you to pray for a long time and often. He wills this delay to keep you in a state of humility and self-contempt and to make you realize the value of his graces.
—St. John Eudes (1601–1680)

Anthony entreated the vision that appeared, saying, "Where were you? Why didn't you appear in the beginning, so that you could stop my distresses?" And a voice came to him: "I was here, Anthony, but I waited to watch your struggle. And

now, since you persevered and are not defeated, I will be your helper forever, and I will make you famous everywhere."
—St. Athanasius (c. 296–373), from *The Life of Anthony*

Never give up prayer, and should you find dryness and difficulty, persevere in it for this very reason. God often desires to see what love your soul has, and love is not tried by ease and satisfaction.
—St. John of the Cross (1542–1591)

In Line with God's Will

Acts 1:4-8, 12-14, 21-22, 24-26; 2:1-4

⁴While staying with them [Jesus' apostles], he ordered them not to leave Jerusalem, but to wait there for the promise of the Father. "This," he said, "is what you have heard from me; ⁵for John baptized with water, but you will be baptized with the Holy Spirit not many days from now."

⁶So when they had come together, they asked him, "Lord, is this the time when you will restore the kingdom to Israel?" ⁷He replied, "It is not for you to know the times or periods that the Father has set by his own authority. ⁸But you will receive power when the Holy Spirit has come upon you; and you will be my witnesses in Jerusalem, in all Judea and Samaria, and to the ends of the earth.". . .

¹²[After Jesus' ascension] they returned to Jerusalem from the mount called Olivet, which is near Jerusalem, a sabbath day's journey away. ¹³When they had entered the city, they went to the room upstairs where they were staying, Peter, and John, and James, and Andrew, Philip and Thomas, Bartholomew and Matthew, James son of Alphaeus, and Simon the Zealot, and Judas son of James. ¹⁴All these were constantly devoting themselves to prayer, together with certain women, including Mary the mother of Jesus, as well as his brothers. . . .

²¹[Peter said,] "So one of the men who have accompanied us during all the time that the Lord Jesus went in and out among us, ²²beginning from the baptism of John until the day when he was taken up from us—one of these must become a witness with us to his resurrection." . . . ²⁴Then they prayed and said, "Lord, you know everyone's heart. Show us which one of these two you have chosen ²⁵to take the

place in this ministry and apostleship from which Judas turned aside to go to his own place." ²⁶And they cast lots for them, and the lot fell on Matthias; and he was added to the eleven apostles.

¹When the day of Pentecost had come, they were all together in one place. ²And suddenly from heaven there came a sound like the rush of a violent wind, and it filled the entire house where they were sitting. ³Divided tongues, as of fire, appeared among them, and a tongue rested on each of them. ⁴All of them were filled with the Holy Spirit and began to speak in other languages, as the Spirit gave them ability.

For the apostles, Jesus' final instructions to them before his ascension had a bittersweet quality. His resurrection appearances and future promises filled them with hope. But his order to stay in Jerusalem, where he had been crucified and where their lives were in constant danger, must have been difficult to accept. In fact, it prompted their immediate question, "Lord, is this the time when you will restore the kingdom to Israel?" (Acts 1:6). They feared what might happen to them next. Although Jesus' reply didn't allay their immediate fears, it did promise future empowerment and victory (see 1:8). With their expectancy heightened, the apostles had the courage to return to the same upper room where they had hid during Jesus' persecution and death.

By naming each of the eleven apostles, Luke shows that the original apostolic band was intact, obedient, and committed to fulfilling the promises of Christ. Jesus proved his divine nature of love by going to the cross, and he affirmed his divine will by appearing to them after his resurrection so they could build the church in his name. He also solidified the trustworthiness of his divine promises by rising from the dead and empowering his apostles with the Holy Spirit. Now it was their turn to respond by praying, waiting, and acting expectantly.

Verse 14 confirms that they prayed: "All these were constantly devoting themselves to prayer." And although uncertain about what the future held, the apostles expected that God would be true to his will, to his nature, and to his promises. God would supply whatever was needed to grow the church and ensure that it would prevail. The apostles acted on that expectation by selecting an eyewitness to replace Judas Iscariot.

What conclusions can we make based on the apostles' actions in this passage? We can pray expectantly, rooted in the conviction that God will answer our prayers according to his will, his nature, and his promises. This expectant faith is founded on God and of what we know of his divine will, nature, and promises. God gives us expectant faith, and he affirms it when he answers our prayers.

We must be careful, however. If our expectations come from ourselves and not from God, we might presume that we can obligate God to answer our prayer, even if it is in contradiction to his will, his nature, or his promises. And we know that sometimes our expectations are a result of selfish or misguided desires, not his divine will. We must also be careful that we only expect God to act in accord with his nature of love. He will not answer prayers that are motivated by retribution or hatred, since that would violate his nature.

We do know that Christ died, rose, and will return in glory to achieve his Father's will—that all who believe in him might come to salvation and have everlasting life. He promises us forgiveness, healing, wisdom, justice, truth, righteousness, his power, his gifts, and his continued presence. We can confidently pray for anything that is truly based on these key promises.

Remember, we cannot overwhelm God with our expectations. We must avoid the stumbling blocks of demanding to understand everything about God's ways or waiting for the right "feelings" before we approach him. He never reprimands us for asking too much of him, but he does chide us for asking too little or not asking at all.

Understand!

1. What was the political climate in Jerusalem that prompted the apostles' question, "Lord, is this the time when you will restore the kingdom to Israel?" What does the question tell you about the apostles' personal concerns?

_____

_____

_____

_____

_____

_____

_____

2. Jesus said the apostles would be baptized with the Holy Spirit. Do you think they had any idea what he meant? Why or why not?

_____

_____

_____

_____

_____

3. What significance did choosing someone to replace Judas Iscariot have for the future of the Church? What did that action say about the expectations the apostles had regarding their ministry?

_____

_____

_____

_____

_____

_____

4. Why did Luke mention each of the eleven apostles and Mary, the mother of Jesus, by name? (see Acts 1:13-14). What implications can we draw from the sequence of the names listed?

_____

_____

_____

_____

_____

_____

5. Why do you think it was important for the apostles and Mary to devote themselves constantly to prayer? What do you think were the benefits of them praying together rather than individually?

_____

_____

_____

_____

_____

_____

▶In the Spotlight
Politics, Perception, and Faith

Jesus often spoke of the kingdom of God. But his hearers perceived the kingdom of God in political rather than in spiritual terms. The Jews were clearly aware of their status as God's chosen people and their destiny for special privilege. But their rebellion against God often put them in the hands of such foreign captors as the Babylonians, Persians, Greeks, and Romans. They longed for the day when the promised Messiah would overpower their enemies and restore them to the political status and independence they formerly enjoyed. This was a key reason why Judas Iscariot turned traitor. He came to realize that Jesus was not willingly going to lead his nation into battle against Roman rule, and so he tried to force him into action. After Pentecost, the apostles came to understand the faith message Jesus preached and worked for the kingdom to take root in the hearts of all.

Grow!

1. How did the expectant prayer of Jesus' followers help to spread the gospel and build the church? How might expectant prayer help you, personally, to build God's kingdom?

_____

_____

_____

_____

_____

_____

2. The apostles asked the Lord to help them choose another apostle. When have you asked the Lord to help you make an important decision? How did it turn out? Are there any pending decisions about which you could ask God?

_____

_____

_____

_____

_____

_____

3. What expectations might God have of you? How can you recognize what these expectations might be? How have you acted on these expectations?

_____

_____

_____

_____

_____

_____

_____

_____

4. Have you ever hesitated in asking God for something? If so, what stopped you from asking? How do you think God might want you to approach him with your needs?

_____

_____

_____

_____

_____

_____

_____

_____

5. Do you ever have doubts that God's power can manifest itself in and through you? What actions and attitudes might help transform passive faith into expectant faith?

_____

_____

_____

_____

_____

_____

▶ In the Spotlight
The Expectant Prayer of an Eight-Year-Old

Our friend Joyce has a serious asthma problem. Her medication usually controls the asthma, but it worsens during climate changes, stress, and allergy season. One day a few friends, including Joyce and her eight-year-old daughter Laura, were at our house, and Joyce began wheezing and coughing. When the asthma reaches such a serious level, Joyce's only relief is to release the phlegm that has built up in her lungs. We were all getting uncomfortable with Joyce's asthma attack when Laura came up behind her, put her hands on Joyce's head, and prayed, "Lord Jesus, make my mother throw up. Amen."

Immediately after her "Amen," Laura turned and ran for the front door.

I asked, "Laura, where are you going?"

She answered, "I don't want to be around when it happens."

As Laura was heading toward the door, her mom ran in the other direction to the bathroom. Doubt or deliberation never entered Laura's mind. She knew that God loved her mother and had provided relief for her asthma in the past. Acting on that knowledge, Laura expected that what God did before he could do again. Expectation was her hope, and prayer was the means of obtaining what she hoped for. May we have the same, childlike faith of Laura, to pray, act, and expect an answer!

Reflect!

1. Reflect on and list the positive attributes that built the expectant faith of the apostles and of eight-year-old Laura. Then list some of the attitudes and actions that may hinder your growth in expectant faith. In prayer, ask the Lord how you can become more expectant in your faith.

2. Read and reflect on the following passages to help increase your understanding of praying expectantly:

> Seeing a fig tree by the side of the road, [Jesus] went to it and found nothing at all on it but leaves. Then he said to it, "May no fruit ever come from you again!" And the fig tree withered at once. When the disciples saw it, they were amazed, saying, "How did the fig tree wither at once?" Jesus answered them, "Truly, I tell you, if you have faith and do not doubt, not only will you do what has been done to the fig tree, but even if you say to this mountain, 'Be lifted up and thrown into the sea,' it will be done. Whatever you ask for in prayer with faith, you will receive."
>
> —Matthew 21:19-22

> When John [the Baptist] heard in prison what the Messiah was doing, he sent word by his disciples and said to him, "Are you the one who is to come, or are we to wait for another?" Jesus answered them, "Go and tell John what you hear and see: the blind receive their sight, the lame walk, the lepers are cleansed, the deaf hear, the dead are raised, and the poor have good news brought to them. And blessed is anyone who takes no offense at me."
>
> —Matthew 11:2-6

> "What no eye has seen, nor ear heard,
>   nor the human heart conceived,
>   what God has prepared for those who love him."
>
> —1 Corinthians 2:9

> Martha said to Jesus, "Lord, if you had been here, my brother would not have died. But even now I know that God will give you whatever you ask of him."
>
> —John 11:21-22

When [Jesus] entered Capernaum, a centurion came to him, appealing to him and saying, "Lord, my servant is lying at home paralyzed, in terrible distress." And he said to him, "I will come and cure him." The centurion answered, "Lord, I am not worthy to have you come under my roof; but only speak the word, and my servant will be healed."

—Matthew 8:5-8

▶In the Spotlight
Contemporary Voices: God's Promises

Even with the best of intentions, we may fail to fulfill our promises because of circumstances beyond our control. But even if we fail or others fail us—even if unforeseen circumstances bring misfortune our way—we still have good reason to hope as Christians. That hope is sure because it is founded on God's faithful promises which have been recorded in the Scriptures.

Put simply, God is *always* faithful. Unlike us he has limitless power and authority, and he backs up every promise he makes with his integrity. Whatever God has promised, we can be certain that he will fulfill it at the appropriate time.

—**Carmen Rojas,** *The Catholic Book of Bible Promises*

Act!

Exercise expectant faith by praying to yield fully to the power of the Holy Spirit, whom you received in the Sacraments of Baptism and Confirmation. Then ask the Lord to reveal how he would want you to be his witness and discuss appropriate action with a trusted friend or spiritual director.

▶In the Spotlight
From the *Catechism of the Catholic Church*

Because the Holy Spirit is the anointing of Christ, it is Christ who, as the head of the Body, pours out the Spirit among his members to nourish, heal, and organize them in their mutual functions, to give them life, send them to bear witness, and associate them to his self-offering to the Father and to his intercession for the whole world. Through the Church's sacraments, Christ communicates his Holy and sanctifying Spirit to the members of his Body. (739)

"The Spirit helps us in our weakness; for we do not know how to pray as we ought, but the Spirit himself intercedes with sighs too deep for words" (Romans 8:26). The Holy Spirit, the artisan of God's works, is the master of prayer. (741)

Trusting the Lord with Your Inner Secrets

Exodus 32:1-2, 4, 7-11, 12b, 14

¹When the people saw that Moses delayed to come down from the mountain, the people gathered around Aaron, and said to him, "Come, make gods for us, who shall go before us; as for this Moses, the man who brought us up out of the land of Egypt, we do not know what has become of him." ²Aaron said to them, "Take off the gold rings that are on the ears of your wives, your sons, and your daughters, and bring them to me." . . . ⁴He took the gold from them, formed it in a mold, and cast an image of a calf; and they said, "These are your gods, O Israel, who brought you up out of the land of Egypt!". . .

⁷The LORD said to Moses, "Go down at once! Your people, whom you brought up out of the land of Egypt, have acted perversely; ⁸they have been quick to turn aside from the way that I commanded them; they have cast for themselves an image of a calf, and have worshiped it and sacrificed to it, and said, 'These are your gods, O Israel, who brought you up out of the land of Egypt!'" ⁹The LORD said to Moses, "I have seen this people, how stiff-necked they are. ¹⁰Now let me alone, so that my wrath may burn hot against them and I may consume them; and of you I will make a great nation."

¹¹But Moses implored the LORD his God, and said, "O LORD, why does your wrath burn hot against your people, whom you brought out of the land of Egypt with great power and with a mighty hand? . . . ¹²Turn from your fierce wrath; change your mind and do not bring disaster on your people." . . . ¹⁴And the LORD changed his mind about the disaster that he planned to bring on his people.

This Scripture passage presents a model for empowering our intercessory or personal prayer because it helps us to see into the heart of Moses. The great prophet undoubtedly knew the gravity of the Israelites' sin of worshipping the golden calf, which had prompted God's anger. But instead of trying to defend them or justify their actions, Moses cried out from his heart for their rescue. His petition appealed to the justice and mercy of God and was motivated by love for the people he had freed from Egypt's slavery. The Lord's favorable answer benefited the Israelites, God's chosen people, and brought glory and honor to God—key prerequisites for effectively praying the desires of our heart.

This account of Moses speaking his heart's desire, despite God's fatal threat, should prompt us to ask a few crucial questions: What motivates the prayer of our heart? If God granted our "heart cry," would it bring him glory and honor? How can we rightly form the attitudes and trust necessary to pray the desire of our heart and be pleasing to God?

Moses' example offers three principles for incorporating and applying this biblical model of praying the desires of our hearts.

First, it is God, not us, who initiates, accomplishes, and empowers what we ask for. Adopting this disposition frees us from the uncertainty of how or what to pray and increases our confidence in the Lord's ability to do what we cannot. Recall that Moses reminded God it was he, not Moses himself, who brought the people out of Egypt (see Exodus 32:11). God had initiated that rescue, and Moses appealed that his mercy toward them would continue.

Second, intimacy with God compels us to speak the desire of our heart, even if what we ask seems impossible. When the Lord revealed his intent to wipe out the idol worshippers (see Exodus 32:10), Moses countered by reminding him of his covenant promise to multiply Abraham's descendants and not destroy them. He knew by experience that righteousness, truth, and loving kindness were an integral part of the heart and nature of God and relied on his intimate relationship as a child of God who longed to please his creator. Therefore, he trusted that God wanted to hear the yearning of his heart.

Third, we should pray with passion rather than resignation. Moses could have submitted himself passively to God's will without a challenge, as Noah did when God told him he would destroy the earth with a flood (see Genesis 6:11-22). He could have reasoned, "You are God, you know everything; whatever your will is, that is what you are going to do. Thy will be done!" But Moses had a deep investment in the Israelites. He championed them in battle against their oppressors and fathered, nurtured, and counseled them on the seemingly endless journey through the desert. His zealous passion for the people impelled him to speak the desire of his heart rather than resign himself to God's expressed intent. Moses prayed the desire of his heart, "And the LORD changed his mind about the disaster that he planned to bring on his people" (Exodus 32:14).

Praying our deepest desires is a positive act of trust and faith in God and may require an adjustment of our attitude and transformation of our will to conform to the truths revealed in Scripture. But once learned and applied, it will liberate us to speak as freely to the Lord as we would to a most intimate friend, confessor, or soul mate. Our hearts will have a new passion, and a God-driven desire will motivate our prayer life.

Understand!

1. Why do you think Aaron submitted to the people's demand to build the golden calf? Why did the people say the golden calf, and not the Lord, had brought them out of the land of Egypt?

   _____

   _____

   _____

   _____

   _____

   _____

   _____

2. Why do you think God called the people "stiff-necked"? What do you think he meant by that term?

   They refused to bow to Gods Commands

   _____

   _____

   _____

   _____

   _____

3. Why was Moses so passionate about saving the people from destruction? What risks was he taking by challenging God?

   Moses had invested a great deal of effort on behalf of the Israelites. He didn't want God to punish and abandon them. God could have punished Moses for daring to disagree with him

4. In his conversation with the Lord, Moses pointed out that God had rescued the people "with great power and with a mighty hand" (Exodus 32:11). How did this argument sway God and help to change his mind?

God may have remembered his promises to abraham Isaac and Jacob and really wanted to fulfill them.

5. Based on the conversation that Moses had with God, how would you characterize their relationship?

Moses was bold in beseeching God to change his mind. God must have known Moses was sincere in his desire for the Jewish people, not for himself

▶In the Spotlight
Moses, Christ, and the Law

Moses is the most dominant biblical figure recorded in the Hebrew Scriptures. His intimacy with God was so deep that only Aaron, his mouthpiece, could speak the messages God gave to him. The importance of Moses as lawgiver is highlighted by five separate codes reflecting Mosaic Law in the Old Testament: (1) The Ten Commandments (see Exodus 20:1-

17); (2) the Law of the Covenant (see Exodus 20:22-23:19); (3) the Code of Priests (see Exodus 25-31); (4) the Law of Holiness (see Leviticus 17–22); and (5) the Code of Behavior (Deuteronomy 12–16).

In the return of Christ from Egypt (see Matthew 2:15), and Christ's baptism in the Jordan (see Matthew 3:13-17), St. Matthew saw Christ as the new Israel and the new Moses. Christ's forty days in the desert (see Matthew 4:1-11) recalled both the forty years of Israel's testing in the desert and the forty days Moses spent on Mount Sinai (see Exodus 24:18). The first Moses, Israel's great lawgiver, presented his people with the law promulgated on Mount Sinai. Christ, the new Moses, presented his law in the Sermon on the Mount (see Matthew 5–7).

Grow!

1. A "desert" experience can be valuable and draw us closer to God or, as was the case with the Israelites, it can make us feel like giving up. Recall a spiritual desert experience in your life. How did you cope with it? How helpful was it to your prayer life?

_____

_____

_____

_____

_____

_____

_____

_____

2. What "gods" are popular in our culture? In what ways might these false gods prevent you from knowing yourself or God in a deeper way? What can you do to counter this temptation in your life?

_____

_____

_____

_____

_____

_____

3. Have you ever prayed the desire of your heart to challenge God's will and intent or despite evidence of little hope for a favorable outcome? If yes, what did you learn? If no, what was your reaction? Did you ever feel like God gave you a reason for not granting your request?

_____

_____

_____

_____

_____

_____

4. How can fear of disappointment prevent us from asking God for what we deeply desire? Write down any fears that might inhibit you. Then share ways to counter such fears.

_____

_____

_____

_____

_____

_____

5. Spend some time praying so that you can discover the deepest desire of your heart. Is it something you have prayed for passionately? If your prayer has not been answered, how might God be calling you to exchange your own desires for his?

_____

_____

_____

_____

_____

_____

_____

▶In the Spotlight
The Desire of a Mother's Heart

Michelle, a seventeen-year-old member of our church in Tennessee, was in a serious automobile accident and was taken eighty miles by helicopter to the University Hospital in Chattanooga. An early diagnosis revealed that she lost a large quantity of blood and had a prolonged deprivation of oxygen to her brain. After almost three hours, the chief neurosurgeon came to the waiting room and told Michelle's parents, her brother, our pastor, and me that her injuries were extremely serious and that we should not get our hopes up that Michelle might survive. He said she was in a deep coma and had severe internal bleeding and brain stem damage. If by some miracle she should survive, he said, she might be in a vegetative state for the rest of her life.

I asked Michelle's mother what the desire of her heart was for her daughter. Through her grief and tears, she said, "I want Michelle to be well and to return to me just like she was before." As she finished speaking those words, I said, "Jesus Christ can heal her brain stem and her other injuries as well.

We need to pray now." Eight of us, including the neurosurgeon and some staff, held hands and prayed the prayer Michelle's mother expressed from the desire of her heart.

When someone you love receives a prognosis that is hopeless, your thoughts and prayers can easily be conflicted. You want a miraculous recovery, but if death seems imminent, you don't want their suffering prolonged. Should you pray for a speedy, painless, and peaceful death, or that God's will be done, or simply pray the desire of your heart? For Michelle's family, praying the desire of their hearts relieved the stress and tension of wondering how or what to pray and established early on that their reliance was on the Lord. In the months that followed, with Michelle still in a deep coma and little hope being offered by her caregivers, the family and many others continued praying the desire of a mother's heart.

About four months after the accident, Michelle awoke from the coma, and one month later she graduated with her high school class. Shortly afterward, she walked with her own strength down the aisle at St. Alphonsus Church to receive the Lord in Communion. Today, Michelle is married and has a child of her own. The desire of a mother's heart and communal prayer united to bring about a miracle that only a few had the courage to openly proclaim, and many hoped for in the quiet recesses of the heart.

Reflect!

1. Reflect on the difference between praying with the passionate desires of your heart or praying in a passive, resigned way. Make a case in writing for adopting the former attitude.

2. To aid your understanding of praying the desire of your heart, read and reflect on the following:

In the garden of Gethsemane, awaiting the arrival of the soldiers who would lead him to crucifixion, Jesus expressed both the desire of his heart and his trust in God. He prayed, "Abba, Father, for you all things are possible; remove this cup from me; yet, not what I want, but what you want" (Mark 14:36).

The first chapter of the First Book of Samuel describes the story of Hannah, wife of Elkanah. Hannah was barren and Elkanah's other wife, Peninnah, used to provoke her because Hannah had no children. Hannah prayed the desire of her heart: "O LORD of hosts, if only you will look on the misery of your servant, and . . . give to your servant a male child, then I will set him before you as a nazarite until the day of his death" (1 Samuel 1:11). Hannah conceived and bore a son and named him Samuel. He became a prophet of the Lord during the days of King David (see 1 Samuel 1:1-28).

> Take delight in the LORD,
>   and he will give you the desires of your heart.
> —Psalm 37:4

The good person out of the good treasure of the heart produces good, and the evil person out of evil treasure produces evil; for it is out of the abundance of the heart that the mouth speaks.

—Luke 6:45

Shun youthful passions and pursue righteousness, faith, love, and peace, along with those who call on the Lord from a pure heart.

—2 Timothy 2:22

▶In the Spotlight
Contemporary Voices: The Father's Love

The Father's love
Is the hope
You can count on:
The first help
In your last
Desperate minutes.

The Father's love
Is the song
You hear on
The radio that
Makes you
Cry for forgiveness.

It is the touch
Or spoken hug
You receive on
Days you feel
Isolated, convicted
To be in solitary
Confinement in the world.

The Father's love
Is the green
Light to go on
With your life
When the world shouts:
No.

The Father's love
Leads to a prayer

Unlike any ever
Said aloud in a church.
It is a doxology
Of our close
Relationship to Abba.
A secret so intimate
We can trust
Only Him with it.

The Father's love
Never stops
Even when we
Think it might
Or should.

It goes on.

—**Philip C. Kolin,** "The Father's Love"

Act!

Start an intercessory prayer group, either in person or online. Invite people to express their needs and hearts' desires, and pray accordingly. Use testimonies of answered prayer to encourage one another.

▶In the Spotlight
From the Wisdom of the Saints

Free your mind from all that troubles you, God will take care of things. Trust in him, I beg you and you will have the fulfillment of what your heart desires.
—**St. Vincent de Paul (c. 1580–1660)**

God accepts our desires as though they were of great value. He accepts our petitions for benefits as though we were doing him a favor.

—St. Gregory Nazianzen (c. 329–c. 389)

We can tell him all the secrets of our heart, disclosing our miseries to him who alone can remedy them.

—St. Margaret Mary Alacoque (1647–1690)

The essence of prayer is therefore the spiritual lifting of the heart toward God. The mind in the heart stands consciously before the face of God, and begins to pour itself out before him.

—St. Theophan the Recluse (1815–1894)

Prayers: —
Helen Bresnahan
Bud Sinner
Janice Miller + Bob
Celebration of Christmas for all
Jacob Hauser + family.
The Baumlers

Learning to Pray "On the Spot"

Acts 3:1-10; 4:13

[1]One day Peter and John were going up to the temple at the hour of prayer, at three o'clock in the afternoon. [2]And a man lame from birth was being carried in. People would lay him daily at the gate of the temple called the Beautiful Gate so that he could ask for alms from those entering the temple. [3]When he saw Peter and John about to go into the temple, he asked them for alms. [4]Peter looked intently at him, as did John, and said, "Look at us." [5]And he fixed his attention on them, expecting to receive something from them. [6]But Peter said, "I have no silver or gold, but what I have I give you; in the name of Jesus Christ of Nazareth, stand up and walk." [7]And he took him by the right hand and raised him up; and immediately his feet and ankles were made strong. [8]Jumping up, he stood and began to walk, and he entered the temple with them, walking and leaping and praising God. [9]All the people saw him walking and praising God, [10]and they recognized him as the one who used to sit and ask for alms at the Beautiful Gate of the temple; and they were filled with wonder and amazement at what had happened to him. . . .

[4:13]Now, when they [leaders of the Sanhedrin] saw the boldness of Peter and John they realized they were uneducated and ordinary men, they were amazed and recognized them as companions of Jesus.

The Jewish day began at six in the morning and ended at six in the evening. For the devout Jew, there were three hours designated for prayer: nine in the morning, twelve noon, and three in the afternoon. Of course, a Jew could pray anytime and anywhere, but tradition and custom taught that prayer in the temple was especially efficacious. Although Peter and John experienced a new empowerment and a new faith at Pentecost, they did not reject their tradition of going to the temple to pray. Rather, Pentecost gave them a new compassion, desire, and sense of urgency to emulate Jesus with the gifts they had received. To the beggar's request for alms, Peter responded, "I have no silver or gold, but what I have I give you" (Acts 3:6).

Peter's words challenge us to reflect on how often we focus more on what we do not have than on what we do have. What Peter "had not" was timidity, fear, or doubt. What he "had" were the gifts of the Spirit: wisdom, knowledge, faith, healing, mighty deeds, prophecy, and discernment of spirits (see 1 Corinthians 12:4-10). Peter understood that these are "on the spot" gifts, to be directed and manifested when and where the Spirit wills. The Spirit requires only a willing vessel to work through.

We have all been in situations where a need was either obvious or expressed. How do we respond? The courageous among us may say something compassionate like, "I can see you are hurting, and I will pray for you." Or we may promise, as we are walking away, "I'll be sure to put you on our prayer list." The timid person may promise to pray for a person in need, but would be more comfortable not vocalizing their prayer. Then there are those who know they should pray but forget soon after learning of the need.

Praying on the spot for a personal petition will keep you in frequent communication with the Lord. It will help you avoid procrastination or laziness that can hinder praying and taking action in faith.

Intercession, including when we pray on the spot for the needs of another, is a deliberate, committed decision that is an integral part of discipleship. Failure or unwillingness to pray for someone in need could stifle the gifts you possess and hinder the work of the Holy Spirit in the life of a person to whom God has given you an opportunity to minister. When you decide to "pray on the spot" for the needs of another, you are bringing that person into an encounter with the Lord. You are not responsible for the results of that encounter. Just delight in being a channel through which God's grace can flow, and trust Jesus to take it from there.

The miraculous healing of the lame man at the Beautiful Gate caused a great stir among the people and their leaders. Because of it, the Sanhedrin, a group of Jewish leaders made up of priestly families and the lay aristocracy, interrogated Peter and John. Peter took no personal credit for the healing but assured his interrogators that it was accomplished in the name of Jesus Christ. Having made themselves enemies of Jesus, the Sanhedrin would have dearly loved to refute any claim of a miracle in his name. But faced with overwhelming evidence and impressed by Peter's boldness, they accepted the authenticity of the healing miracle (see Acts 4:16).

Understand!

1. Peter takes center stage in the miraculous healing of the crippled beggar. What do you think was the role of John? Why was his presence important?

_____

_____

_____

_____

_____

_____

_____

2. List some things Peter "had" to give the crippled beggar. What was the most important?

_____

_____

_____

_____

_____

_____

3. What was significant about the lame beggar's actions after he was healed? Why do you think he reacted in that way?

_____

_____

_____

_____

_____

_____

_____

4. Peter followed up the healing with preaching about Jesus (see Acts 3:11-26). How did the healing miracle set the stage for the people to believe what he said?

_____

_____

_____

_____

_____

_____

_____

5. What attributes of Peter and John caused the Sanhedrin to be amazed? Why?

_____

_____

_____

_____

_____

_____

▶In the Spotlight
The Beautiful Gate

The "Beautiful Gate" was on the eastern front of the temple (facing the Mount of Olives). By far the most magnificent of all temple gates, it was 50 cubits high and 40 cubits wide (75 feet high and 60 feet wide). It was made of Corinthian brass, carved and covered with plates of gold and silver. It was so heavy that it required twenty men to move it. According to the Jewish historian Josephus (37–c. 101), among the signs that were seen as a premonition of the destruction of the Temple was that the gate opened of itself one midnight about the year 30 B.C. Because people coming to the temple to pray and worship were generous to those in need, beggars chose to sit at this gate since it was the most used.

Grow!

1. The devout Jew prayed many times in a given day. How often do you pray each day? Would you like to pray more often? Brainstorm for ways you could pray more often throughout the day, even while you are busy with other activities.

_____

_____

_____

_____

_____

_____

_____

_____

2. Which gifts of the Spirit (see 1 Corinthians 12:4-10) would you describe as "on the spot" gifts? Which have you used most often? Not as often? Why?

_____

_____

_____

_____

_____

_____

_____

_____

3. What obstacles prevent you from praying boldly? What attitudes or actions might help you to overcome these obstacles?

_____

_____

_____

_____

_____

_____

_____

_____

4. Why do you think it is important to exercise our spiritual gifts? What do you think happens if we fail to put them to use?

_____

_____

_____

_____

_____

_____

_____

_____

5. Has anyone ever prayed for you in a bold or persistent way? What were the effects? What was your reaction to that prayer?

_____

_____

_____

_____

_____

_____

_____

_____

▶In the Spotlight
Put "On the Spot" for God

I was serving as an usher at an ecumenical conference, standing to the right of the main platform and listening to the keynote speaker. There was a large speaker box in front of me, and next to that a group of about twenty deaf people and a "signer" who interpreted what the speaker was saying. The speaker had finished his presentation and an announcer introduced a music group on-stage. As I was about to leave that area, a "signer" approached me and, pointing to the ribbon I was wearing that identified me as a conference volunteer, said, "Oh, good, you're a team member. There's a girl here, deaf from birth, who wants someone to pray for her to receive her hearing." I said, "Okay, I'll go find someone and be right back." She said, "No, *you* have to pray." She held my arm and motioned to another "signer" to bring the deaf girl to me.

Soon the girl, about sixteen years old, was standing in front of me with a signer on each side of me, waiting for me to pray. A large crowd had gathered to see what was happening. I was not prepared for this challenge to exercise faith so boldly and publicly and felt uneasy about being put on the spot. My first thought was to tear off my volunteer's badge and run, but the signer had a firm hold on my arm. I closed my eyes, took a deep breath, and prayed inwardly, "Come, Holy Spirit, empower your servant." Then, I put my hands over the girl's ears and prayed, "In the name of Jesus Christ, receive your hearing. Amen." The girl immediately began to screech because for the first time she heard the sound of the (loud) music coming from the large speaker box near us. Those who knew the girl confirmed that she had been deaf from birth and began praising God for the miracle of her being able to hear.

Reflect!

1. Reflect on the times you were put "on the spot" for God. How did you react? What gifts of the Holy Spirit did you call on to use? If you failed to act, what thoughts or attitudes would help you in the future?

2. The following passages will help you adopt the disposition of praying boldly:

> [Jesus said], "I will do whatever you ask in my name, so that the Father may be glorified in the Son. If in my name you ask me for anything, I will do it."
>
> —John 14:13-14

> What good is it, my brothers and sisters, if you say you have faith but do not have works? Can faith save you? If a brother or sister is naked and lacks daily food, and one of you says to them, "Go in peace; keep warm and eat your fill," and yet you do not supply their bodily needs, what is the good of that? So faith by itself, if it has no works, is dead.
>
> —James 2:14-17

> For this reason I remind you to rekindle the gift of God that is within you through the laying on of my hands; for God did not give us a spirit of cowardice, but rather a spirit of power and of love and of self-discipline.
>
> —2 Timothy 1:6-7

When I came to you, brothers and sisters, I did not come proclaiming the mystery of God to you in lofty words or wisdom. . . . . I came to you in weakness and in fear and in much trembling. My speech and my proclamation were not with plausible words of wisdom, but with a demonstration of the Spirit and of power, so that your faith might rest not on human wisdom but on the power of God.

—1 Corinthians 2:1, 3-5

We know love by this, that he laid down his life for us—and we ought to lay down our lives for one another. . . . . Little children, let us love, not in word or speech, but in truth and action.

—1 John 3:16, 18

▶In the Spotlight
A Lesson from Pope John Paul II

An American archbishop, in a television interview a few days after the death of Pope John Paul II, recalled a time in Rome when he was walking with the Holy Father and a cardinal from the Vatican joined them. The cardinal told them that he had a difficult and troubling decision to make. So the pope stopped and, after listening intently to the problem, commanded that the three pray on the spot.

How often do we fail to respond immediately to the needs of others because our faith is too timid or we are too busy? Despite his busy life Pope John Paul II demonstrated that praying was too grave a responsibility to put off; it could not wait.

Act!

Make a commitment to the Lord to speak, act, and pray boldly for his glory. Each day for the next two weeks ask God to send someone to you who is in need of prayer. Be alert and attentive for the answer and the opportunity. When the person comes, act by praying on the spot. Record the response, the results, and your feelings about stepping out in faith to exercise God's gift of healing.

▶In the Spotlight
"Bold Speech"

Parrhesia is a word used in the New Testament to mean "bold speech." Luke uses the word in Acts 4:13, when the Jewish leaders describe the "boldness" of Peter and John. The *Catechism of the Catholic Church* says *parrhesia* is a "beautiful, characteristically Christian expression" that can be defined as "straightforward simplicity, filial trust, joyous assurance, humble boldness, the certainty of being loved" (2778). Here are other Scripture passages where the term *parrhesia* is used:

Of this gospel I have become a servant according to the gift of God's grace that was given me by the working of his power. . . . This was in accordance with the eternal purpose that he has carried out in Christ Jesus our Lord, in whom we have access to God in boldness [*parrhesia*] and confidence through faith in him.

—Ephesians 3:7, 11-12

Beloved, if our hearts do not condemn us, we have boldness [*parrhesia*] before God; and we receive from him whatever we ask, because we obey his commandments and do what pleases him. . . . All who obey his commandments abide in him, and he abides in them. And by this we know that he abides in us, by the Spirit that he has given us.

—1 John 3:21-22, 24

Let us therefore approach the throne of grace with boldness [*parrhesia*], so that we may receive mercy and find grace to help in time of need.

—Hebrews 4:16

Stepping Out in Faith

Mark 10:46-52

⁴⁶As he and his disciples and a large crowd were leaving Jericho, Bartimaeus son of Timaeus, a blind beggar, was sitting by the roadside. ⁴⁷When he heard that it was Jesus of Nazareth, he began to shout out and say, "Jesus, Son of David, have mercy on me!" ⁴⁸Many sternly ordered him to be quiet, but he cried out even more loudly, "Son of David, have mercy on me." ⁴⁹Jesus stood still and said, "Call him here." And they called the blind man, saying to him, "Take heart; get up, he is calling you." ⁵⁰So throwing off his cloak, he sprang up and came to Jesus. ⁵¹Then Jesus said to him, "What do you want me to do for you?" The blind man said to him, "My teacher, let me see again." ⁵²Jesus said to him, "Go; your faith has made you well." Immediately he regained his sight and followed him on the way.

J esus and his disciples were leaving Jericho on their way to Jerusalem, about eighteen miles southwest, to celebrate the Passover feast. This was to fulfill the law, which required that every male Jew over twelve years of age who lived within a day's journey of Jerusalem come to the city for Passover.

Everywhere Jesus went, people gathered to hear the wisdom and comfort of his words and to receive his healing touch. This day was no exception. As Jesus and his disciples walked the Jericho road, a crowd gathered around him. A blind beggar, Bartimaeus, took his usual position on the road to beg alms from pilgrims on their way to Jerusalem. It was customary for those who were unable to attend the feast to line the streets of towns and villages through which groups of Passover pilgrims passed so they could gather around the popular rabbis to hear their teaching on the way. Bartimaeus heard the clamoring of the crowd and asked who was passing by. When he learned it was Jesus, he called out in desperation, "Jesus, Son of David, have mercy on me!" By addressing him as Son of David, the blind man was publicly identifying Jesus as King of the Jews, the Messiah.

Imagine the shock of the multitudes when Jesus stopped the entourage to hear the cry of one sinful beggar! In doing so, Jesus fulfilled Psalm 34:6, "This poor soul cried, and was heard by the LORD, and was saved from every trouble." Bartimaeus, now the center of attention, had to face the hostile crowd and became so frightened that he needed encouragement to step forward. The disciples provided that courage: "Take heart; get up, he is calling you" (Mark 10:49). As Bartimaeus' hope for healing was stirred, he threw off his cloak, sprang up, and walked to Jesus. Because a beggar collected alms in the fold of his coat, throwing away his cloak symbolized complete abandonment of his old way of life. He would have to beg no more—the treasure of heaven awaited him.

When this blind man, standing in front of Jesus, heard, "What do you want me to do for you?" he must have thought it an odd question. But Jesus always had a reason for his questions. He knew what the blind man wanted, and he challenged Bartimaeus's general request, "Jesus son of David, have mercy on me," hoping to stir a more specific request in faith. Jesus' challenge was the spark of increased faith that Bartimaeus needed. Dare he risk disappointment, embarrassment, or rejection by making a specific request? Yes! Bartimaeus quickly understood what the Lord required of him. He rose to the challenge and declared specifically, "Let me see!" And immediately he received his sight.

With the help of Jesus and his disciples, Bartimaeus rose from desperation to courage, from courage to hope, from hope to faith, and from faith to a place in Scripture as one who was healed. But his story doesn't end there. When Jesus said to him, "Go; your faith has made you well," many new possibilities awaited the blind man who could now see. He chose to follow Jesus on the "way" (Mark 10:52), a term used by the early Christian community to describe their way of life (see Acts 9:2).

Once a beggar who could do no more than receive, Bartimaeus was now a disciple, empowered to give. He did not selfishly go his own way after his need was met. He saw and he followed.

Understand!

1. What was it about Jesus that caused crowds to gather around him? Do you think curiosity was a factor? Of the answers you gave, which would you consider to be of greater importance? Why?

_____

_____

_____

_____

_____

_____

2. What do you think stirred the blind beggar's hope for healing and caused him to go from asking for mercy to asking for sight?

_____

_____

_____

_____

_____

3. What would you imagine were the thoughts and attitudes of the crowd when Jesus stopped the entire procession to pay attention to the blind beggar? If you were in the crowd, what might you have thought about Bartimaeus' cry to Jesus and Jesus' response?

_____

_____

_____

_____

_____

_____

4. What roles did the following play in the blind beggar's healing?

The blind man:_____

The crowd:_____

The disciples:_____

Jesus:_____

5. In what ways did Bartimaeus receive more than physical sight from his encounter with Jesus? What do you think is the most significant result of the story of the blind beggar? Why?

_____

_____

_____

_____

_____

_____

_____

_____

▶In the Spotlight
Passover: Feast of Freedom and Covenant

Jesus healed Bartimaeus on the way to Jerusalem to celebrate the feast of Passover, which commemorates the birth of the Jewish nation. Rescued from slavery, this wandering tribe of nomads was free to become a nation that would serve the living and true God. Moses' words declared God's saving action, "The LORD will pass through to strike down the Egyptians; when he sees the blood [of the sacrificial Lamb] on the lintel and on the two doorposts, the LORD will pass over that door and will not allow the destroyer to enter your houses to strike you down" (Exodus 12:23). The sacrificial lamb in Exodus prefigured the promised Messiah. As John the Baptist saw Jesus coming toward him, he appropriately declared, "Here is the Lamb of God who takes away the sin of the world!" (John 1:29).

Grow!

1. Do you ever feel that it is difficult to get Jesus' attention? What specific actions could you take when you pray that might help you to feel as if Jesus has heard you?

_____

_____

_____

_____

_____

_____

_____

2. How hopeful are you that Jesus can heal a physical, emotional, or spiritual wound that you or someone you love is suffering? How specific have you been in asking for that healing?

_____

_____

_____

_____

_____

_____

_____

3. How would you describe to someone the risks of praying for a specific request or outcome from God? Do the benefits outweigh the risks? Why or why not?

_____

_____

_____

_____

_____

_____

_____

4. Name a specific incident in which you moved from desperation to courage, from courage to hope, and from hope to faith? How did you see God act in response to your faith?

_____

_____

_____

_____

_____

_____

5. After his sight was restored, Bartimaeus decided to follow Jesus. Looking back on your life, can you recall a specific moment or period of time when you made a choice to follow Jesus rather than going your own way? If so, how did your life change? If not, how might such a deliberate decision affect you?

_____

_____

_____

_____

_____

_____

▶In the Spotlight
A Specific Prayer Answered

Here is a story from an excited parishioner who had just learned about the need to pray specifically:

"We could not find Boots, our cat, and the whole family was upset. So I called everyone together, thinking, 'What the heck, maybe praying for a specific need works.' I told them, 'We're going to pray to find Boots. Let's hold our hands, bow our heads, and close our eyes.' I made the sign of the cross and said, 'Lord

Jesus, bring Boots home to us. Amen.' We opened our eyes, and to our amazement, Boots was right there in front of us."

It was obvious that praying specifically and receiving an immediate answer was a new experience for this man and his family. It wasn't that they hadn't prayed before, but their new attitude of prayer differed from praying for grandma to feel well or for world peace. Such prayers are general, and ones in which we rarely look for an answer. If grandma actually had a day that her arthritis was not causing pain or discomfort, credit would go to the medications she was taking rather than to a general prayer. And who searches the news every hour for a favorable reply to a prayer asking for world peace?

While finding a cat may not qualify as a mountain-moving experience for some, it was an important faith event for the members of this family, who gained confidence in the Lord and learned a new way to pray.

Reflect!

1. Think about what worries have been occupying your mind lately. Which particular concerns might move you to pray specifically?

2. Reflect on praying specifically in the following passages:

> When the disciples saw Jesus walking on the sea, they were terrified, saying, "It is a ghost!" And they cried out in fear. But immediately Jesus spoke to them and said, "Take heart, it is I; do not be afraid."
>
> Peter answered him, "Lord, if it is you, command me to come to you on the water." [Jesus] said, "Come." So Peter got out of the boat, started walking on the water, and came toward Jesus.
>
> —Matthew 14:26-29

One day, as we were going to the place of prayer, we met a slave-girl who had a spirit of divination and brought her owners a great deal of money by fortune-telling. While she followed Paul and us, she would cry out, "These men are slaves of the Most High God, who proclaim to you a way of salvation." She kept doing this for many days. But Paul, very much annoyed, turned and said to the spirit, "I order you in the name of Jesus Christ to come out of her." And it came out that very hour."

—Acts 16:16-18

Then Elijah said to all the people, "Come closer to me"; and all the people came closer to him. First he repaired the altar of the LORD that had been thrown down; Elijah took twelve stones, according to the number of the tribes of the sons of Jacob, to whom the word of the LORD came, saying, "Israel shall be your name"; with the stones he built an altar in the name of the LORD. Then he made a trench around the altar, large enough to contain two measures of seed. Next he put the wood in order, cut the bull in pieces, and laid it on the wood. He said, "Fill four jars with water and pour it on the burnt offering and on the wood." Then he said, "Do it a second time"; and they did it a second time. Again he said, "Do it a third time"; and they did it a third time, so that the water ran all around the altar, and filled the trench also with water.

At the time of the offering of the oblation, the prophet Elijah came near and said, "O LORD, God of Abraham, Isaac, and Israel, let it be known this day that you are God in Israel, that I am your servant, and that I have done all these things at your bidding. Answer me, O LORD, answer me, so that this people may know that you, O LORD, are God, and that you have turned their hearts back." Then the fire of the Lord fell and consumed the burnt offering, the wood, the stones, and the dust, and even licked up the water that was in the trench. When all the people saw it, they fell on their faces and said, "The Lord indeed is God; the Lord indeed is God."

—1 Kings 18:30-39

One of the criminals who were hanged there kept deriding [Jesus], and saying, "Are you not the Messiah? Save yourself and us!" But the other rebuked him, saying, "Do you not fear God, since you are under the same sentence of condemnation? And we indeed have been condemned justly, for we are getting what we deserve for our deeds, but this man has done nothing wrong." Then he said, "Jesus, remember me when you come into your kingdom." [Jesus] replied, "Truly I tell you, today you will be with me in Paradise."

—Luke 23:39-43

Elijah was a human being like us, and he prayed fervently that it might not rain, and for three years and six months it did not rain on the earth. Then he prayed again, and the heaven gave rain and the earth yielded its harvest.

—James 5:17-18

▶In the Spotlight
Obstacles to Prayer

St. Augustine cautioned against yielding to a casual, general, or unfocused attitude on prayer when he said, "The prayer of Egyptian monks was sudden and ejaculatory so that the intense application so necessary in prayer should not vanish or lose its keenness by a slow performance."

Our communication with God should be more intense than most other activities we engage in, and nothing should be more important to us than prayer at the moment of need. The intensity and focus of our prayer should increase as the need becomes more critical, causing us to focus specifically on the need and on God, who always acts in our favor.

Act!

The blind beggar threw off his cloak as an act of complete abandonment of his old way of life. Make an honest assessment of your habits, negative attitudes and emotions, and sins, and take specific action to change the direction of your life. Each day, ask Jesus specifically to help you with an attitude or sin. Record in a prayer journal how he answered your prayer.

►In the Spotlight
From the *Catechism of the Catholic Church:*
The Jesus Prayer

Bartimaeus' cry to Jesus has been repeated by millions of Christians through the centuries. It is known as the "Jesus Prayer."

The urgent request of the blind men, "Have mercy on us, Son of David" or "Jesus, Son of David, have mercy on me!" has been renewed in the traditional prayer to Jesus known as the *Jesus Prayer*: "Lord Jesus Christ, Son of God, have mercy on me, a sinner!" Healing infirmities or forgiving sins, Jesus always responds to a prayer offered in faith: "Your faith has made you well; go in peace." (2616)

The name of Jesus is at the heart of Christian prayer. All liturgical prayers conclude with the words "through our Lord Jesus Christ." The *Hail Mary* reaches its high point in the words "blessed is the fruit of thy womb, Jesus." The Eastern prayer of the heart, the *Jesus Prayer*, says: "Lord Jesus Christ, Son of God, have mercy on me, a sinner." Many Christians, such as St. Joan of Arc, have died with the one word "Jesus" on their lips. (435)

The invocation, "Lord Jesus Christ, Son of God, have mercy on us sinners" . . . combines the christological hymn of *Philippians* 2:6-11 with the cry of the publican and the blind men begging for light. By it the heart is opened to human wretchedness and the Savior's mercy. (2667)

Preparing for Battle and Living Victoriously

Ephesians 6:10-18a

[10]Finally, be strong in the Lord and in the strength of his power. [11]Put on the whole armor of God, so that you may be able to stand against the wiles of the devil. [12]For our struggle is not against enemies of blood and flesh, but against the rulers, against the authorities, against the cosmic powers of this present darkness, against the spiritual forces of evil in the heavenly places. [13]Therefore take up the whole armor of God, so that you may be able to withstand on that evil day, and having done everything, to stand firm. [14]Stand therefore, and fasten the belt of truth around your waist, and put on the breastplate of righteousness. [15]As shoes for your feet put on whatever will make you ready to proclaim the gospel of peace. [16]With all of these, take the shield of faith, with which you will be able to quench all the flaming arrows of the evil one. [17]Take the helmet of salvation, and the sword of the Spirit, which is the word of God. [18]Pray in the Spirit at all times in every prayer and supplication.

God loves us so much that he created us with the freedom to return that love by the attitudes and actions of our lives. Satan, on the other hand, wants to enslave us to sin. "Satan or the devil and the other demons are fallen angels who have freely refused to serve God and his plan. Their choice against God is definitive. They try to associate man in their revolt against God" (*Catechism*, 414). When we recognize attitudes or actions in our lives that play into Satan's plans, corrective measures are in order.

St. Paul, who was no stranger to persecution or the "wiles (the use of tricks to deceive someone) of the devil," wrote to the Ephesians from a prison cell. His prison guards were Roman soldiers wearing full armor, which suggested to him that Christians have armor as well. So he used the metaphorical prescription of the "armor of God" to help us recognize and defeat Satan's attacks, describing the various parts of the soldier's armor in Christian terms.

Unlike the Roman soldier who relies on his own strength, the Christian draws strength from God's power through union with Christ. God makes the armor available to the believer, who then must put it on. Facing daily temptations, trials, and attacks without first putting on our armor is akin to going out in a torrential rainstorm without clothes or umbrella and expecting our skin not to get wet. So what armor do we need to "put on"?

1. *Truth as a belt around your waist.* The belt, which held the soldier's tunic and his sword, provided him freedom of movement. Jesus said, "You will know the truth, and the truth will make you free" (John 8:32). Knowing Jesus, the way, truth, and life, as Lord and redeemer combats the bondage of deceit and self-doubt and allows us to act freely as his witnesses.

2. *Righteousness [right conduct] as a breastplate.* A breastplate protects the chest area, which contains the heart. In biblical language, the heart is the seat of a person's rational and emotional activity. Forces of evil can attack our decisions, conduct, and emotions and destroy our relationship with God. Our new life in the Spirit—a life in which we live in Christ and Christ lives in us—gives us the grace to act righteously and protects us from evil.

3. *Shoes for your feet to proclaim the gospel of peace.* Peace is not the absence of war or freedom from troubles. It is the assurance that our circumstances are in the hands of God. Peace produces tranquility, confidence, and contentment, equipping us to proclaim the good news of our transformation in Christ.

4. *Take the shield of faith to quench the flaming arrows of the evil one.* The Roman soldier carried a large, oblong shield made of two sections of wood glued together. When the enemy's fiery dart hit the shield, it sank into the wood and extinguished the flame. Like the shield, faith is clinging closely to the Lord and believing and acting on his promises, no matter how hot the flames of temptation or persecution roar.

5. *Take the helmet of salvation.* Without a covering for our head, we are most vulnerable to physical, emotional, and spiritual attacks that would attempt to rob us of salvation. The hope of salvation is the eternal glory awaiting those who "have washed their robes and made them white in the blood of the Lamb" (see Revelation 7:13-17). Salvation's hope is our bulwark against short-term or temporary attacks.

6. *Take the sword of the Spirit, which is the word of the Lord.* The sword is both a defensive and an offensive weapon. Jesus quoted the Scriptures to defeat the assaults and temptations of

Satan in the desert (see Matthew 4:1-10). We can never win God's battles with our own thoughts and ideas—we must know and use God's word.

7. *Prayer, the greatest weapon of all.* Pray to honor God by the proof of your life, offer up your petitions, and pray for your family, friends, and spiritual and political leaders.

By putting on these seven forms of protection, the armor of God will cover us fully from head (helmet) to toe (sandals). Fear or worry about evil has no place in the life of the Christian. Jesus has already defeated the evil one. He wants us to live victoriously and provides everything we need to do so, but we need to remain ever vigilant and prepared for battle to counter our own weaknesses.

Understand!

1. What terms does Paul use to describe the "wiles of the devil" (Ephesians 6:11)? Why do you think Paul says the Christian struggle is against the devil and not other human beings?

_____

_____

_____

_____

_____

_____

2. How would you describe the general tone of Paul's message in this passage? Would it be positive and encouraging or negative and worrisome? Explain your answer. What does it tell you about St. Paul as an individual and as a church leader?

_____

_____

_____

_____

_____

3. What did Paul mean by the statement, "Put on the *whole* armor of God" (Ephesians 6:11; emphasis mine)? Why would it be insufficient to "put on" only part of God's armor?

_____

_____

_____

_____

_____

4. What does the image of flaming arrows suggest regarding temptation and persecution? How can this image help you the next time you are experiencing temptation?

_____

_____

_____

_____

_____

_____

_____

5. Why do you think Paul called the word of God "the sword of the Spirit" (6:17)? How can God's words in Scripture really act as a weapon against evil in our lives?

_____

_____

_____

_____

_____

_____

_____

▶In the Spotlight
The Legend of St. Christopher

Catholic author Bert Ghezzi, writing on the power of the cross to defeat Satan, recounts a legend popular in the Middle Ages about St. Christopher:

Christopher, a magnificent giant, left home in search of the most powerful king in the world so that he could serve him.

On his travels he first met a great Christian king and pledged to follow him. One day a jester entertained the royal court with a song about the devil, and every time the king heard the word "devil," he made the sign of the cross. Puzzled by this strange gesture, Christopher asked the king what it meant. "Whenever I hear the devil mentioned," said the king, "I defend myself with this sign for fear that he might get some power over me and do me harm."

"If you are afraid of the devil," said Christopher, "he must be stronger and greater than you. So goodbye! I am going to look for the devil and enter into his service because he must be the most powerful king on earth."

A short time later, as Christopher was walking along a road, he met a large army. Their leader, a formidable-looking warrior, asked him where he was going. Christopher said, "I'm searching for the devil. I want to take him as my master."

"I'm the one you're looking for," said the warrior. Glad to have found the devil, Christopher promised to serve him and join his army. As the army continued its march, they passed a roadside cross. When the devil noticed it, he was terrified and hid behind a boulder. Shocked by his new master's behavior, Christopher asked him what made him so afraid. The devil . . . said, "Once a man named Jesus Christ was nailed to a cross, and when I see his sign, it fills me with terror, and I run from it."

"If that's the case," said Christopher, "then this Jesus is greater and more powerful than you. Therefore, I still haven't found the greatest king on earth. So I'm leaving you. I'm going to search for Christ and make him my master."

Later in the story, Christopher finds Christ while he is working as a ferryman, carrying people across a river. He takes Christ as his king and serves him even in martyrdom.

—**Bert Ghezzi,** *The Sign of the Cross*

Grow!

1. We need to prepare ahead for the attacks of Satan, which are sure to come. What practical things could you do each day to prepare you for these onslaughts?

   _____

   _____

   _____

   _____

   _____

   _____

2. Share an instance when you felt you were in a struggle with "the spiritual forces of evil" (Ephesians 6:12) mentioned by Paul. When did you realize that you were in the struggle? How were you able to be victorious?

   _____

   _____

   _____

   _____

   _____

   _____

3. What does it mean to you to live a new life in the Spirit? How does the Holy Spirit help us to fight off temptation?

   _____

   _____

   _____

   _____

   _____

   _____

4. In what areas of your life are you most susceptible to the lies and doubts that Satan may plant in your mind—your marriage, your job, your parenting abilities, your confidence? In those moments when you are experiencing doubts, why is it important to stand on the truth?

_____

_____

_____

_____

_____

_____

_____

5. How open are you to asking other Christians to pray with you when you are under a spiritual attack? How would the sacraments aid you in your struggle?

_____

_____

_____

_____

_____

_____

_____

_____

►In the Spotlight
Instructions and Encouragement from Prison

During St. Paul's imprisonment in Rome from A.D. 61 to 63, he wrote letters to the Ephesians, Philippians, Colossians, and to Philemon, which the church considers inspired and includes in the canon of New Testament books. Whatever circumstances he encountered, Paul remained an example of faithfulness to the Lord and to his ministry. The overriding messages of his "captivity letters" are a contrast to what one would expect from a prisoner, beaten and in chains. Paul's "good news" proclaims the lordship and sovereignty of Jesus, the value of Christian community, and encouragement and instructions on prayer, joy, faith, and daily conduct.

Paul's endearing and encouraging words express the peace, joy, and contentment of a disciple fully committed to Jesus, ready to die for his cause. The "captivity letters" reflect a life dedicated completely to Christ, regardless of conditions or circumstances. Paul's priorities and attitude of the heart overcame any internal or external human constraints he had to endure.

Reflect!

1. We are to be aware of evil in our world and arm ourselves against Satan, who wants to separate us from the Lord's person and works. But evil should not frighten, overcome, or debilitate us. Prayer in the name of Jesus empowers us as disciples of the Lord to triumph over evil in every form. Reflect on a social evil that damages society, such as abortion or poverty. Dedicate yourself to praying for God to overcome that evil, and ask the Lord to give you direction on what actions you can take personally to combat it.

2. Read and reflect on the following passages to help increase your understanding of praying with the full armor of God:

Jesus called seventy disciples and sent them to preach the good news: heal the sick, and drive out demons. On returning the disciples reported the success of their mission. "The seventy (disciples) returned with joy, saying, "Lord, in your name even the demons submit to us!"" (Luke 10:17).

> The night is far gone, the day is near. Let us then lay aside the works of darkness and put on the armor of light.
> —Romans 13:12

> Submit yourselves therefore to God. Resist the devil, and he will flee from you. Draw near to God, and he will draw near to you.
> —James 4:7-8a

> The Lord will take his zeal as his whole armor, and will arm all creation to repel his enemies.
> —Wisdom 5:17

> [Jesus said], "Stay awake and pray that you may not come into the time of trial; the spirit indeed is willing, but the flesh is weak."
> —Matthew 26:41

▶In the Spotlight
Praying Psalm 91

Psalm 91 contains defensive, offensive, and instructional elements and, like all the psalms, can benefit our prayer life. Verses of the Psalm are in italics. A sample prayer to use follows the verses.

You who live in the shelter of the Most High, / who abide in the shadow of the Almighty, / will say to the LORD, *"My refuge and my fortress; / my God, in whom I trust."*

Father, you are Almighty God, higher than any other. In you I take refuge from the storms, temptations, and trials of this day. You are a fortress of protection around me, keeping me from all harm.

For he will deliver you from the snare of the fowler/ and from the deadly pestilence; / he will cover you with his pinions, / and under his wings you will find refuge; / his faithfulness is a shield and buckler.

I thank you, Lord, for your faithfulness, assuring me that you are always vigilant in your protection and strength.

You will not fear the terror of the night, / or the arrow that flies by day, / or the pestilence that stalks in darkness, / or the destruction that wastes at noonday.

I thank you for delivering me from fear in every hour of the day, regardless of the time or fierceness of the attack. I intercede in prayer for (mention specific names and circumstances) and ask that you deliver them from fear, give them your peace, and draw them closer to you.

A thousand may fall at your side, / ten thousand at your right hand, / but it will not come near you. / You will only look with eyes / and see the punishment of the wicked. Because you have made the LORD *your refuge, / the Most High your dwelling place, / no evil shall befall you, / no scourge come near your tent. / For he will command his angels concerning you / to guard you in all your ways. / On their hands they will bear you up, / so that you will not dash your foot against a stone.*

Lord, I receive your promises of deliverance. In the name of Jesus, I rebuke anything that may harm me and my loved ones. I receive with gratitude the presence of your angels guarding my every movement. Protect also (mention specific names and circumstances of those who are presently in harm's way).

You will tread on the lion and the adder, / the young lion and the serpent you will trample under foot.

I receive the empowerment of your Spirit and pray that I will boldly confront and defeat the forces of evil that would attack me and those for whom I pray.

Those who love me, I will deliver; / I will protect those who know my name. / When they call to me, I will answer them; / I will be with them in trouble, / I will rescue them and honor them. / With long life I will satisfy them, / and show them my salvation.

I love you, Lord, and desire to remain faithful in my love for you. Gently correct my faults and failings. Rescue me from poor choices and decisions, guilt and pride. Give me the joy of your salvation. Hear and answer this prayer through the power of the name of Jesus Christ, who lives and reigns with you, Father, and the Holy Spirit, one God forever and ever, Amen.

Act!

The Psalms are a "school of prayer." They represent the full range of human experiences in very personal and practical ways. They provide not only models to follow but also inspire us to voice our deepest feelings and aspirations to God. The Psalms fit the times, seasons, and patterns of our life and are adaptable to our moods, needs, and experiences. Whatever is happening and at whatever moment of time; we can turn to the psalms for solace, wisdom, and protection.

Practice praying the Psalms using the example from Psalm 91. Then teach someone to pray what you have learned. Be guided by the following key psalm references:

- When you feel affliction (stress, trials, problems):
  Pray Psalms 3, 27, 31, 54, 62, 70, 91, 124.

- To praise and thank God:
  Pray Psalms 23, 65, 92, 118, 134, 136, 150.

- For intercessory prayer:
  Pray Psalms 20, 67, 122, 132.

- For instruction and guidance:
  Pray Psalms 1, 5, 25, 73, 112, 127, 131.

▶In the Spotlight
St. Bernadette, Warrior for Christ

Although only fourteen years old when the Blessed Virgin Mary appeared to her, Bernadette Soubirous (1844–1879) was a warrior for Christ. St. Bernadette saw and heard the Virgin Mary at Lourdes, France. She was canonized not for her visions themselves but for the patience and trust she exhibited through the trials she endured because of the visions. Considering herself a soldier of the faith, she wrote, "I know that soldiers have a lot to endure. If upon rising they would only take the trouble to say to our Lord every morning this tiny prayer: 'My God, I desire to do and to endure everything today for the love of thee,' what glory they would heap up for eternity."

Practical Pointers for Bible Discussion Groups

A Bible discussion group is another key that can help us unlock God's word. Participating in a discussion or study group—whether through a parish, a prayer group, or a neighborhood—offers us the opportunity to grow not only in our love for God's word but also in our love for one another. We don't have to be trained Scripture scholars to benefit from discussing and studying the Bible together. Bible-study groups provide environments in which we can worship and pray together and strengthen our relationships with other Christians. The following guidelines can help a group get started and run smoothly.

Getting Started

- Decide on a regular time and place to meet. Meeting on a regular basis allows the group to maintain continuity without losing momentum from the previous discussion.

- Set a time limit for each session. An hour and a half is a reasonable length of time in which to have a rewarding discussion on the material contained in each of the sessions in this guide. However, the group may find that a longer time is even more advantageous. If it is necessary to limit the meeting to an hour, select sections of the material that are of greatest interest to the group.

- Designate a moderator or facilitator to lead the discussions and keep the meetings on schedule. This person's role is to help preserve good group dynamics by keeping the discussion on track. He or she should help ensure that no one monopolizes the session and that each person—especially shy or quiet individuals—is offered an opportunity to speak. The group may want to ask members to take turns moderating the sessions.

- Provide enough copies of the study guide for each member of the group, and ask everyone to bring a Bible to the meetings. Each session's Scripture text and related passages for reflection are printed in full in the guides, but you will find that a Bible is helpful for looking up other passages and cross-references. The translation provided in this guide is the New Revised Standard Version: Catholic Edition. You may also want to refer to other translations—for example, the New American Bible or the New Jerusalem Bible—to gain additional insights into the text.

- Try to stay faithful to your commitment and attend as many sessions as possible. Not only does regular participation provide coherence and consistency to the group discussions, it also demonstrates that members value one another and are committed to sharing their lives with one another.

Session Dynamics

- Read the material for each session in advance and take time to consider the questions and your answers to them. The single most important key to any successful Bible study is having everyone prepared to participate.

- As a courtesy to all members of your group, try to begin and end each session on schedule. Being prompt respects the other commitments of the members and allows enough time for discussion.

If the group still has more to discuss at the end of the allotted time, consider continuing the discussion at the next meeting.

- Open the sessions with prayer. A different person could have the responsibility of leading the opening prayer at each session. The prayer could be a spontaneous one, a traditional prayer such as the Our Father, or one that relates to the topic of that particular meeting. The members of the group might also want to begin some of the meetings with a song or hymn. Whatever you choose, ask the Holy Spirit to guide your discussion and study of the Scripture text presented in that session.

- Contribute actively to the discussion. Let the members of the group get to know you, but try to stick to the topic, so that you won't divert the discussion from its purpose. And resist the temptation to monopolize the conversation, so that everyone will have an opportunity to learn from one another.

- Listen attentively to everyone in the group. Show respect for the other members and their contributions. Encourage, support, and affirm them as they share. Remember that many questions have more than one answer and that the experience of everyone in the group can be enriched by considering a variety of viewpoints.

- If you disagree with someone's observation or answer to a question, do so gently and respectfully, in a way that shows that you value the person who made the comment, and then explain your own point of view. For example, rather than say, "You're wrong!" or, "That's ridiculous!" try something like, "I think I see what you're getting at, but I think that Jesus was saying something different in this passage." Be careful to avoid sounding aggressive or argumentative. Then, watch to see how the subsequent discussion unfolds. Who knows? You may come away with a new and deeper perspective.

- Don't be afraid of pauses and reflective moments of silence during the session. People may need some time to think about a question before putting their thoughts into words.

- Maintain and respect confidentiality within the group. Safeguard the privacy and dignity of each member by not repeating what has been shared during the discussion session unless you have been given permission to do so. That way everyone will get the greatest benefit out of the group by feeling comfortable enough to share on a deep, personal level.

- End the session with prayer. Thank God for what you have learned through the discussion, and ask him to help you integrate it into your life.

The Lord blesses all our efforts to come closer to him. As you spend time preparing for and meeting with your small group, be confident in the knowledge that Christ will fill you with wisdom, insight, and grace and the ability to see him at work in your daily life.

Sources and Acknowledgments

Session 1: Praying Persistently

"The Legal System of First-Century Palestine" based on William Barclay's *The Daily Study Bible Series*, The Gospel of Luke, (Louisville, KY: Westminster John Knox Press, 1975).

"Pray without Ceasing" from "The Call to Unceasing Prayer," an article by Henri J. M. Nouwen, appearing in *Sojourners* Magazine, August 1980.

Quotation of Blessed Jean Eudes taken from *Quotable Saints* by Rhonda DeSola Chervin, (Ann Arbor, MI: Servant Publications, 1992), 158.

Quotation of St. Athanasius from *The Wisdom of the Saints, An Anthology* by Jill Haak Adels (New York City: Oxford University Press, 1989), 60.

Quotation of St. John of the Cross from *The Quotable Saint*, by Rosemary Ellen Guiley (New York City: Checkmark Books, 2002), 217.

Session 2: Praying Expectantly

"Contemporary Voices: God's Promises" from *The Catholic Book of Bible Promises* by Carmen Rojas (Ann Arbor, MI: Servant Books, 1988), viii.

Session 3: Praying the Desire of Your Heart

"The Father's Love," from *Deep Wonder: Poems* by Philip C. Kolin (Grey Owl Press, 2000), 96–97. Used with permission.

Quotation of St. Vincent de Paul from *Letters* quoted in *Saint of the Day* by Leonard Foley, OFM, ed. (Cincinnati: St. Anthony Messenger Press, 1990), 248.

Quotation of St. Gregory Nazianzen from *Saint of the Day* by Leonard Foley, OFM, ed. (Cincinnati: St. Anthony Messenger Press, 1990), 9.

Quotation of St. Margaret Mary Alacoque from *The Quotable Saint* by Rosemary Ellen Guiley (New York City: Checkmark Books, 2002), 212.

Quotation of St. Theophan the Recluse from *The Quotable Saint,* by Rosemary Ellen Guiley (New York City: Checkmark Books, 2002), 215.

Session 4: Praying Boldly

"The Beautiful Gate" based on the article "The Temple of Jerusalem," *Catholic Encyclopedia,* accessed at http://www.newadvent.org/cathen/14499a.htm.

Session 5: Praying Specifically

Quotation from St. Augustine in "Obstacles to Prayer" from *The Wisdom of the Saints, An Anthology* by Jill Haak Adels (New York City: Oxford University Press, 1989), 39.

Session 6: Praying with the Full Armor of God

"The Legend of St. Christopher" from *The Sign of the Cross: Recovering the Power of the Ancient Prayer* by Bert Ghezzi (Chicago: Loyola Press, 2004), 82–83. Reprinted with permission of Loyola Press. To order copies of this book, call 1-800-621-1008 or visit www.loyolabooks.org.

Quotation of St. Bernadette from *Quotable Saints* by Rhonda DeSola Chervin (Ann Arbor, MI: Servant Publications, 1992), 191.

Also in The Word Among Us Keys to the Bible Series

Item# BTWAE5

Treasures Uncovered: The Parables of Jesus
A Six-Week Bible Study for Catholics
by Jeanne Kun

This popular six-session Scripture guide will help you explore the surprising—and often challenging—dimensions of six of Jesus' parables. Fascinating historical details, explanations of the Greek root words used in the original gospels, and quotations from church fathers included.

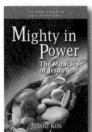

Item# BTWBE6

Mighty in Power: The Miracles of Jesus
A Six-Week Bible Study for Catholics
by Jeanne Kun

This Scripture guide will help you understand the miracles of Jesus as invitations to experience God's mercy and salvation today. Each of the six sessions includes questions for delving into the miracles of Jesus and applying them to daily life. Suitable for individuals or groups.

Item# BTWCE7

Food from Heaven: The Eucharist in Scripture
A Six-Week Bible Study for Catholics
by Jeanne Kun

Food from Heaven will help you understand and appreciate the biblical foundations of the Mass, and especially of the Eucharist. Among the passages studied are Old Testament stories that foreshadow the Eucharist, along with gospel scenes that bring Jesus' own teaching to life.

To order call 1-800-775-9673
or order online at www.wordamongus.org